Oh, to be Kept by Jesus

Betty Jessie Maddox

Copyright © 2018 Betty Jessie Maddox

All rights reserved. No part(s) of this book may be reproduced, distributed or transmitted in any form, or by any means, or stored in a database or retrieval systems without prior expressed written permission of the author of this book.

ISBN: 978-1-5356-1556-3

PROSE AND POETRY BY THE author; special submissions by Shonda J. Wheeler, Kamryn Jessie, Tazanya d. Maddox (daughter, on-high), Flora Maddox Reid (aunt, on-high); and artwork by Eric M. Maddox.

Contents

Preface 1
Reclaiming My Heritage, Our Charge 3
Our Marriage BLESSED by God 9
Our Lives Ordered by God 12
Recognizing the BLESSINGS, IN SPITE OF 21
Kept by God's POWERFUL HAND 28
Some *Nos* Are a Blessing in Disguise 31
I/We Can Overcome, NO MATTER WHAT! 38
Led by His Spirit... 44
Empowered by God's PEACE,
His GRACE, and His MERCY 49
To Encourage You, Too.. 54

Preface

God says, "I know the plans I have for you. NOT to HARM you, PLANS for GOOD, a FUTURE with HOPE" (Jeremiah 29:11–14). Oh, how I wish we ALL understood this and studied His Word in which He ALSO said what He would do IF we'd keep our minds stayed on Him, TRUSTING Him, TRULY LOVING Him. If we are walking in His guidance, His Word, we'll be AMAZED at the AWESOME ways that He will show up and show out in our lives and on our behalf. We often take sooo much for granted, without putting forth the effort to fully understand, appreciate, and receive ALL that our God had in mind for us when He created us and said, "That's good!" I pray that I have done Him justice herein as I share how He has shown up and has shown out in my life and that of my family. I wish that I could just open you up and pour it into your very spirit. WHAT IS JUST AS AWESOME A THOUGHT IS THE FACT THAT, UPON REALLY LOOKING BACK OVER YOUR LIFE, YOU, TOO, COULD SAY THE SAME.

IF that is not so, let me encourage you to discover that IT IS POSSIBLE to say that same thing.

Come journey with me as I revisit the many times that I/we have been kept and will continue to be so blessed/kept by the POWER of God in many aspects of my/our lives. As you read my testimony of the goodness of God, I pray that you will revisit those moments, perhaps forgotten, in your life as well. If you find them to be few, I further pray that you will seek to cultivate that part of your life that He is just waiting to BLESS BEYOND YOUR WILDEST IMAGINATION— YOUR HEART'S DESIRES. YOU'LL BE AMAZED AND SOOO GRATEFUL ANEW TO REVISIT OR DISCOVER THE EVIDENCE OF HIS LOVE AND DESIRED INVOLVEMENT IN YOUR LIFE, TOO.

Chapter 1

Reclaiming My Heritage, Our Charge

My earliest church life was spent in Cool Springs Baptist Church (near Crawford County, Georgia), where I was baptized at nine years old. Most of my elementary to my pre-college life was spent in Columbus, Georgia, at Shady Grove Baptist Church. If most of us would admit it, when we went off to college, we settled for chapel and very little additional church worship. For us, that spilled over into our early married life, with, perhaps, a visit here and there to St. Mark AME, Aubrey's family's home church.

When we moved to the Ben Hill area, our home was just a half block from a very small church to which I began to go, taking Eric (our firstborn) with me. Because the community was in a transitional period, that church soon left, but by then, I had become reacclimated to church life and sought a real base for our family, hoping all of us (including Aubrey) would soon be reconnected to church-worship experiences. The minister, Brother Paul, of Ben Hill UMC, just about a block or two from our home, came with a transitional church group of black and white membership, which had decided to visit those families moving into the area. I was immediately impressed and felt connectedness to those who represented the church.

So, Eric and I began to become involved there. When I say ***involved,*** I mean really committed to Ben Hill UMC!!! I joined the Sanctuary Choir, and when the Majestic Choir was formed, I became a charter member of it, too. Our first African American Minister was Rev. Cornelius L. Henderson, an AWESOME Man of God, as well. Soon I was involved in the leadership of the church in what seemed like every area possible, from the local United Methodist Women's presidency to involvement in the leadership of the College Park District UMWs, from Lay Speaker to Associate Lay Leader. Soon Aubrey, now a member, and I became Co-Chairs of Family Ministries, members of the Council on Ministries and the Administrative Board. I became first lay teacher of the Couples in Christ Sunday School Class. **HEAD OVER HEELS IN INVOLVEMENT, EVERYWHERE!!!** Aubrey and I had become involved in the founding of the Atlanta Community Gospel Choir, which ministered Black gospel history in churches and parks around Atlanta and even traveled to Missouri and Columbus, Georgia, to minister a concert down memory lane of Black gospel music. I tell you all of this just to say that when we become "committed" to God and His work, look out!!!!! We were even led to begin a community prayer and Bible study group before it was formally started at the church. AND GOD WILL BLESS YOUR SOUL BEYOND ANYTHING YOU COULD EVER IMAGINE, and He will use you in MIGHTY ways, recognizing your contributions to the life of the church!!!

Near the mid-1990s, Rev. Cornelius L. Henderson, recently reappointed our pastor, soon to become Bishop Henderson, was supported in his decision to honor our family with a Maddox Family Day at Ben Hill UMC by our newly appointed pastor, Rev. McCallister Hollins. I must pause here to give buckets of love, not just from us but from many who have been blessed to become a part of the Ben Hill United Methodist Church family. As I often speak of The Vine and our connection to Him and to one another, I PROUDLY SAY THAT BEN HILL UMC IS THE PERSONIFICATION OF THAT CONNECTION, ONE TO ANOTHER AND THE CHURCH'S CONNECTION TO THE VINE. Ben Hill, I praise God for you daily!!! You are an amazing family!!! We came to Ben Hill in 1972 and plan to remain here until glory time!!! HALLELUJAH!!!!

AMEN, AMEN, AMEN!!! TO GOD BE ALL OF THE GLORY, HONOR, AND PRAISE!!! He will honor your commitment in some AWESOME WAYS, ALLOWING YOU FAVOR TO DO, TO BE, TO RECEIVE, AND TO GIVE!!! **That's just the "frosting on the cake"/the sweetness/BLESSINGS He chooses to give for your commitment to His work.** Sometimes this "frosting" is in the way that He keeps us when trouble comes, or when He keeps trouble from coming.

In the late seventies, as I became a more passionate disciple of Christ through more devoted Bible study, I began to watch several television ministries, hungry for more and more of the Word, desiring a closer relationship with God. I remember hearing testimonies of former drug addicts and others who were drastically changed as they developed a relationship with Christ. After one such time, I said, "What a mighty testimony. I wish I had such an AMAZING testimony of the effects of Christ in my life." It was then that I heard so clearly, "It is because I've KEPT YOU all along that you've not needed that type of testimony. Ask your mother about your illness and how I kept you." He then directed me to begin to look back over my life to see that He had kept me so that such a testimony as theirs was not needed.

I soon began to realize what an AWESOME testimony I did, and still do, have as I began to notice, through my spiritual eyes, how often He had indeed kept me (kept me safe, kept me sane, kept me in His joy, kept me in His peace, His mercy, and His grace). For this appointed assignment, to recall and to give testimony of His GOODNESS, I began to wonder what witness to share, BUT THERE WERE SO MANY THAT I COULD NOT DECIDE. So I prayed and asked God which one I should share but heard no answer, except that there have been many times to recall. I began to receive direction relevant to which I should share to show God's GRACE and MERCY, His POWER in our lives.

As I asked for clarification, His will was confirmed by our pastor and then Minister of Music that Sunday at church as they BOTH were led to sing **"Oh, to Be Kept."** And so I attempt here to be obedient.

"Oh, to be kept…" When I was about two years old, Mom went out West to California to find work, and I was left with my grandparents for a while. I suddenly developed a high fever, and they became so concerned that they thought Mom needed to return home, but, just as mysteriously as the fever came, it disappeared. I'm told that they thought that I might have had a rheumatic heart problem, but I've not heard any such concern since and I've led a very active life. It was also interesting to have my mother's mother say that during that time of my illness, my grandfather—my father's father who'd passed—visited me in spirit. I had been told that a time or two before but never after my illness.

"Oh, to be kept..." When I was a senior in high school, while I was asleep one night I began to feel a presence next to my bed but, in that sleep mode, I somehow thought that it was my girlfriend playing with me, and I just retreated farther under the covers. I still felt this presence and peered out only to have a young man, with a knife at my throat, motion me to "shhhhh" at which time I screamed at the top of my voice. He then ran around my sister's bed to our bedroom door and paused. Needless to say, I screamed again, and he ran out of the house. We saw that he'd entered through our bathroom window. After I left for college, I heard that there were other incidents of that nature that occurred in our neighborhood before someone was caught.

Chapter 2

OUR MARRIAGE BLESSED BY GOD

I WAS BLESSED TO BE able to participate in a work-study program as a part of my admission requirement to Morris Brown College in Atlanta, where I met Aubrey during my senior year. He had returned to Morris Brown on an athletic scholarship following a period of military service in the US Air Force. During his service years, he participated on the military's basketball team and had garnered an AWESOME reputation as a point guard. Of course, because he was an excellent player, he had become, in my opinion, a little cocky. Despite this, we became friends, ONLY FRIENDS, and I began to encourage him to be less "full of himself." A month or two after we met, and after one of my friends stopped having a crush on him, we began to date a little. Believe it or not, about a month later (following the Christmas break, during which time he came to Columbus to visit, unbeknownst to his mother, my mother, or even me). Soon after, he called my mom and announced his desire to marry me. Needless to say, since she really did not know him from Adam, she wondered if everything was okay, to which he gave assurance that it was, and to which she gave assurance that she'd be up here on the weekend. SUCH A STRANGE START FOR SUCH AN AMAZING RELATIONSHIP that they began to develop. I STILL DON'T REMEMBER really saying "yes," but I don't remember saying "no," either. I guess I just knew it was to be. AND NOW, **HERE WE ARE, FOUR YEARS BEYOND A HALF CENTURY, STILL TOGETHER, LOVING EACH OTHER MORE, FINISHING EACH OTHER'S THOUGHTS/SENTENCES**, and becoming two who have grown and are still growing in the "REAL" INTIMACY that our Pastor Rev. Dr. Byron E. Thomas recently encouraged couples to develop. But that does not mean that there were not a few times early in our married years, and at a point about fifteen years into our marriage, when **God kept both of us.** I felt that we BOTH were kept when a rush to decision-making could have caused a one- to two-year marriage—and later, a near twenty-year marriage—to come to an end. His grace and His mercy kept both of us. FOR THAT, DEAR HEAVENLY FATHER, WE ARE SOOO GRATEFUL!!!

Yesterday, I found this message that I sent to Aubrey some years ago. I was amazed that its message echoes the sentiments mentioned above, many years later. PRAISE GOD!!!

To Dee Dee, My Husband

I am sooooooooooo **BLESSED** to be a branch connected to **YOU** on that **SPECIAL VINE, *in a SPECIAL WAY*!!!!!!!!** I have come to believe, for many reasons, that we were destined to meet and grow old together, to complete each other's sentences and thoughts, and to love each other unconditionally. **I *thank God for you and the family He BLESSED us to create TOGETHER.*** *I PRAY THAT GOD BLESSES YOU BEYOND YOUR MOST AMAZINGLY POSSIBLE DREAMS AS HE HAS SO DONE FOR ME BY GIVING ME YOU TO LOVE, HONOR, AND APPRECIATE,*

F O R E V E R!!!!!!!!!!

YOUR OTHER HALF, FOREVER!!!!!!!!!!!!!!!!!!
Lilbits

Chapter 3

Our Lives Ordered by God

I mentioned that God took me back in time and caused me to begin to notice, as time continued to pass, just how much He was/is orchestrating our lives. At the point at which I began to desire to grow in my spiritual walk with God, I began visiting Christian bookstores more. On one such visit, I discovered a bookmark with my name on it with the indication that its Christian meaning is "consecrated to God." I was pleased to discover that. Inspired by that, I began to desire to know the meanings of the names of the other members of We 5 (Aubrey, me, Eric, Kirk, and Tazanya). At that point, I did not spend much time searching, but more than thirty years later, I was prompted to look again (for about the third time), and what I found that I could not find before then was ASTONISHING!!

Oh, to be Kept by Jesus

Back in 1965, during my first pregnancy, as I watched television one day, I heard the word "Tazanya." I don't remember if I saw the name or just heard it, but I thought that it was beautiful and decided that, if our firstborn were a girl, that would be her name. I did know that "deAnn" was a nickname for Elizabeth, which is my name. I told Aubrey that he should decide the name if we had a boy. He chose Eric Maurice. As I said before, it took thirty-five-plus years for me to discover that **"Eric" is a nickname for Aubrey**. IMAGINE THAT!!! He had no idea. Aubrey nicknamed all of us: Me–Lilbits (I used to be -Smile); Tazanya—Lilbeaks and Tee; Eric– Rooper; Kirk—Boo; and we all call Aubrey, – Dee Dee (I think from Eric on). With our second child, I told Eric that if the sibling would be a boy, he could name him. Eric chose Kirk Jermaine, **having NO idea that "KIRK" means BROTHER**. By now, I was having church!!!

Now, when Kirk was born, since I was in labor for quite some time, the doctors decided to do a C-section, because they feared, as I was later told, that Kirk might be stillborn should they wait longer. At this time, I decided that perhaps I should give up on using my girl's name and get a tubal ligation so that we would not possibly put another child in danger. But as I procrastinated, God and Tazanya said, "No way!" Now, I have not told you what **I discovered her name to be. Praise God for "God's Grace"!!!** AND SOO SHE WAS/IS!!!!!!!!!!!!!!!!! All of the names for the males mean "kingly" or "stout in power." As I/God began to fashion the name "We 5" for us, I was shown how much of our personalities/gifts are similar. We ALL seem to draw people who trust us for guidance/wisdom (at least in most things), and we all love to sing. God even allowed us several opportunities to sing as a group at PTSAs and one or two other occasions. FIVE PEAS IN A POD!!! —SMILE

We 5: Aubrey, Betty, Eric, Kirk and Tazanya

God kept ALL of us on one occasion when our adventurous two younger children, Kirk and Tazanya (Tee), decided to take a "road trip" while their father worked outside on the car and lawn and I worked inside the house. Aubrey thought that they'd gone inside, while I thought they were outside with him. But, oh no, they'd decided to take a road trip (we suspect that Tee led the decision-making this time). Kirk was around five or six years old and Tee about three or four years old when this happened. A police car pulled up to our house, and the policeman asked Aubrey, "Do you know these people?" Can you imagine the look on his face as he looked into the car and there sat the two world travelers, Tee in the middle? They'd decided to go a little over a half mile up to Campbellton Road, crossing the street to a service station to play with toys. And there they sat when the attendant called the police. I was so thankful that they both knew their address and were able to tell him where they really belonged. I was soooo thankful that I'd not discovered their absence before they were returned to us. I was also very grateful that Department of Family and Children's Services had not been contacted. UPON THINKING OF IT MANY TIMES THEREAFTER, I would be just as thankful to God and His keeping them and us as if it had just happened anew each time. I praise God for His being there every step of the way. We discovered how Mary and Joseph must have felt when, on their way home after their tax-paying trip, twelve-year-old Jesus decided to strike out on his own as he began to embrace his calling; though Jesus was older than our children, you can imagine what our hovering over them thereafter must have been like. Hallelujah!!! Aubrey even denied them permission to visit their grandmom in Columbus without our being in tow.

"Oh, to be kept…" While Eric, our oldest child, was yet a teenager, I was visited by a friend of ours, and when she left, I began praying in my prayer language, thinking that I was praying for her safe travel home. But I was further confused when she arrived home and called yet, I was still prayerful. Obediently, I continued to pray. It was not until several years later at a Watch Night Service that I discovered for whom I'd prayed. It was for Eric, our pastor's daughter, and others, as they'd gone to a fast food establishment. Through our pastor's daughter's testimony about the value of family, I discovered that a person had been there waving a gun in a threatening manner at customers, and when I called and questioned her about the details (time, etc.), it all was true to the time during which the Holy Spirit prayed through me. Thank You, Father God, for Your Spirit!!! THANK YOU, FATHER, FOR PROTECTING HIM/THEM FROM HARM!!!

"Oh, to be kept…" again - **from physical harm.** I was blessed when, in the early nineties, as we prepared for vacation, I went to K-Mart to purchase a few things. As I was about to get in our Explorer, two young men approached, one coming up behind me, placing something against my neck, which he said he would use to "blow my brains out," while the other went to the other side of the car. The guy who had one of his hands over my mouth and the other hand holding a weapon against my neck firmly demanded, "Hurry and unlock the other door!" I was not working to his desired speed as he threatened me again, calling me the "b" word. I said, "I can't see with your hand over my eyes." As he became more agitated, God used the other young man as an angel, as his friend said, "Man, leave the lady alone and hurry up!" Then I was commanded to get down on the ground while they rushed off with my car.

God was there, too, in the young police officer who came to investigate and take me home. That further gave me peace, as I discovered the policeman to be a young man who'd grown up in the apartment above us at our first residency. To make a long story shorter, once I was at home, I became righteously indignant and spoke to Satan, declaring, "You have no business with anything that belongs to me because I am a child of the King!" I claimed my possessions back by name, declaring/demanding, "I want my car back unharmed, my purse, all of my cards, and my keys!!!"

The next day, East Point Police called and asked if I'd lost something recently. I told them of the carjacking, and when I went to the station, they gave me some of the belongings from my purse. They'd fallen out after the two young men had gone to a grocery store and attacked a sixty-five year old lady, who tried to protect her bag, breaking her nose. As they fled, some of my belongings that had been dumped out of the purse fell out of the car. That injury could have occurred to me! But God had kept me!!!!!!

The next day I received a call that there had been an ANONYMOUS CALL to another police station, the caller believing that there were stolen cars in an apartment complex. God is sooo AWESOME!!! It's amazing that all of this took place across three different county jurisdictions. When the police responded to this call, they found my car with **the rear lift door** up and music playing as if someone were about to go somewhere in it. But no one was in it at the time; therefore, they were able to retrieve it UNDAMAGED, WITH ALL OF MY KEYS SCATTERED ABOUT INSIDE. About a day or so later, a young lady, advised by friends NOT to call me because I might think she was involved, called anyway to tell me that she'd found my purse and other belongings from it. She said, "When I found the little card inside your purse that said 'Jesus Loves You,' I decided to risk calling you." At that time, all that I could do was thank her, but God heard my desire to do more. Later, I was able to find her in an UNBELIEVABLE WAY AND BLESS HER AT AN UNBELIEVABLE TIME OF NEED IN HER LIFE. When I was blessed with money (it must have been tax season), I went looking for her where she worked, BUT I was told that she no longer worked at that nursery. I reminded them of how she'd blessed me earlier and indicated that I wanted to bless her financially. Though they were not supposed to do so, they did tell me where she now worked. GOD WAS SO FAITHFUL TO HER TOO. I discovered that she now worked less than two minutes from our home. I went to the nursery to see her and was told that she was outside with the children. Again, I explained why I wanted to see her and they called her in. I again thanked her for the way that she'd blessed me after the carjacking and handed her the token of my appreciation. She began to cry and tell me that she REALLY NEEDED THAT BLESSING. Her mom had told her to lift her concern to God, and He would be faithful to her and answer her need. We hugged and said our goodbyes, BUT I guess you know that I had church on my way home!!! THANK YOU, GOD, FOR USING ME TO BLESS HER!!!

I was further BLESSED AND A BLESSING when I was asked to attend the trial for the young man whom I earlier claimed to be a blessing to me, as he told his companion in crime to leave me alone. I discovered that he was raised by his grandmother, which in itself pointed to some issues. I was asked about his part in the carjacking and was able to speak to that which was good in him. I hope that in some way that testimony helped to begin some significant change in direction for him.

Chapter 4

Recognizing the BLESSINGS, IN SPITE OF

Our daughter, Tazanya, whom God blessed to become all that she had specifically claimed in her life AND MUCH MORE before her homegoing, was a VERY SPECIAL YOUNG LADY whose story God allowed me to share in a book, ***She Graduated Early: from Earth to Glory,*** testifying of God's faithfulness to her, **from the way that He marked the spot of the symptoms of her illness that afterward disappeared to the MANY ACCOMPLISHMENTS she claimed, as she believed that she could do ALL things through Christ,** who strengthened her (Phil. 4:13). She chose to bring God glory and honor through the way she represented Him in character and in determination to become valedictorian of her class to save us money on college. We had our oldest in college, and in another year, our second son would begin his studies. The praises she shared in song, some we would discover to often be prophetic in their testimony to her life's journey, encouraged sooo many.

I had not wanted her to attend my high school but to support the neighborhood school. However, when she became ill, God showed me how the decision she'd desired earlier would now be a blessing, as I would be able to go to the doctor with her, and she and I would then be able to get to school quickly. MORE AMAZING THAN THAT is the fact that Aubrey was informed of a promotion he'd received the Friday BEFORE the Saturday that we discovered the lump in her side. HE HAD NO PRIOR KNOWEDGE OF BEING CONSIDERED FOR PROMOTION from the assembly line to Quality Control, an office position. Now he would be able to take her to the doctor or for chemo, unlike he'd have been able to do on the assembly line at Ford Motor Company. HOW AWESOME IS OUR GOD!!!!

Not only was that a BLESSING as it relates to Tee's needs and my PEACE OF MIND, but later he would represent Ford Motor Company at a car show in New York, singing at Atlanta Motor Speedway, and the celebration of Ford's ranking as the number-one car-manufacturing plant in America. God does not limit His "keeping" to the times when life is rough; He also allows us more moments of JOY to balance out the survival efforts that we hold on to.

Aubrey—Annointed Singer, Counselor, Retired-Ford, Church Leader

Tee's commitment to representing God in ALL that she undertook resulted in MANY RECOGNITIONS. FROM BECOMING VALEDICTORIAN OF HER CLASS, a debater, musical theater lead roles, an inspirational soloist, and a choir member from early elementary school through high school, participating in church and in school. She won many academic and talent awards for performances in debate, language arts, Spanish, math, and music, as well as recognition from her leadership as a McDonald's Young History Makers of Tomorrow and Young Women of Distinction given by United Methodist Women of Ben Hill UMC. She was also a cheerleader from early elementary school through high school. Through her faith in God and His faithfulness toward her, she truly embodied a belief in His Word as the strength of her life. Her faith in God gave me soooo much peace, as I, too, chose to trust Him in ALL things. HER HOMEGOING IN ITSELF WAS A MIRACULOUS WORK OF GOD!!! As I revisited the tape of her service, I could hardly believe the number of students who were led to give their lives to

Tazanya—Annointed Singer, Val, Debater, Actress, Cheerleader

Christ, from her best friend, Haneefah, to what looked like forty to fifty students, **at least.** GOD WAS SOOO GLORIFIED!!! SOOO MAGNIFIED!!!

I promised Him at that moment that I would not allow that indescribable sorrow to steal my joy, **AND HE REALLY TOOK OVER FROM THERE.** During the next week, however, there would be challenges to the peace I'd acquired when the issue of naming another valedictorian arose. Some students and others from other Georgia cities heard, even protested, the pending decision. At that point, I encouraged them to avoid causing chaos in an effort to honor Tee and think instead of how she'd want them to respond. In that light also, I talked with our principal, whose dilemma I could understand, but I also told him that I had no problem with the naming of another valedictorian if Tee were honored, posthumously, for what she'd accomplished. Our principal, Mr. Bibbs, and the Senior Counselor, Mr. Hargrove, announced that Tamika, an amazing young student of mine, would now be promoted from salutatorian to valedictorian. I pray that God was GLORIFIED as he decided to do so and as Mr. Bibbs went a step further in asking me to share some thoughts that she might have shared in her valedictorian address during the graduation ceremony. **HOW AWESOME WAS THAT!!!**

A week or so following her homegoing, I went to the Lincoln Cemetery to share a plaque that she'd won. It was a very hot day, and I was listening to gospel music as I entered the grounds, but I turned it down in reverence to those buried there. I shared with her for a moment and then told her I'd meet her (spirit) back at the house. As I returned to the car, before leaving the grounds, I clearly heard in my spirit, "Turn the radio back up." I did, only to hear, "Hello, Mother, I'm all right now. I made it over, and I'm all right now. I had to cry sometimes, but He wiped the tears from my eyes. Hello, Mother, I'm all right now." I guess you know I had church right then and there!!! I stopped the car and scrambled to find a pen to write the words down because I'd never heard that song before. Later, through investigation, I discovered that it was a real song, **but I never heard it again until I was able to purchase it after** a new shipment arrived. **I played it only once, and to my amazement, it was twice as fast as it was that day at the cemetery.** God allowed me time to catch the words. NOW, I THOUGHT THAT WAS THE END OF IT, BUT as I was driving to Columbus one Saturday, about ten years later, to spend the day with my mother, I thought of Mother's Day and surfed the stations for more gospel music. I found a station on which, JUST AT THAT MOMENT, I BEGAN TO HEAR: "Hello, Mother, I'm all right now. I made it over and I'm all right now…" AGAIN!!! WHAT AN AWESOME MOTHER'S DAY GIFT FROM OUR DAUGHTER, HER GOD, AND OURS!!!

"Oh, to be kept…" About a week after our daughter's homegoing, Kirk, our younger son, had a bad cold. He took some medicine and went about his business that day, BUT at about midnight, he called me to say he could not breathe. I attempted to have him sit up, but he couldn't. Instead, he slid off his bed, onto the floor, and Aubrey called an ambulance while I told the devil "NO!!!" and prayed over Kirk in my prayer language. Because he and Tee were very close, I knew that some of this was brought on by her death, BUT the devil was a liar. Kirk had pneumonia and was diagnosed with some "heart" concerns as well, but he was soon fine. Later when he, against his mother's advice (SINCE HE'D NOT EXERCISED MUCH LATELY), decided to play basketball with his faculty friends, he received an injury that the doctor said might be difficult to mend (because of his size) and might result in a limp. BUT, AGAIN, although there were other issues to develop after that surgery, THE LEG MENDED WELL AND THERE WAS NO LIMP!!!

Chapter 5

Kept by God's POWERFUL HAND

I continue the Maddox men's story here, when a few years later, there was the double Maddox men's visits to the emergency room the weekend of the Majestic Choir's reunion concert. Aubrey had gone to the hospital some time before because of bleeding from a stomach infection, which resulted in his having to have a transfusion. So we thought that when he began to have shortness of breath again, something similar must be going on. But even with my insistence, he decided to try to wait until after the concert and have it checked out.

In the meantime, Eric, who had recently made early-morning visits to the refrigerator and had spoken of smoothies often, had come in from church with smoothies on the brain, again. We'd all decided to rest before the concert. Soon he called me to say that he could not move (having finished a thirty-two-ounce smoothie). I told him to continue to try while I prayed and also tried to convince him to go to emergency room.

He had definite issues with doctors and hospitals but was finally convinced. We took him to the hospital, and since it would take some time for them to do all that they needed to do with him, thinking he'd be okay and leaving soon, we returned home to prepare for the concert and would check back (and pick him up) on the way to the concert. Well, that plan was altered, as they'd not finished, and we went on to the concert, planning to pick Eric up after. Well, Aubrey barely made it through his song when he became too weak and collapsed. Then this persuasion thing had to start all over again. So off we went to the emergency room AGAIN. I TOLD THE NURSE, "I DO NOT PLAN TO MAKE THIS A FAMILY AFFAIR AND JOIN THEM!!!"—each in his own emergency room bed. Well, they found that Eric's blood sugar was 947 **(I've since tried to double-check this count, because it's unbelievable)**. HE'D NEVER BEEN DIAGNOSED DIABETIC BEFORE. IF GOD HAD NOT KEPT HIM AND ME/US, he could have been paralyzed or dead, but PRAISE GOD!!! Eric continues to monitor his diabetes, but God has continued to bless him with FAVOR. He continues to do the work for which God continues to allow him many more years to minister to the young boys of our church, to praise Him through his artistic and musical talents and so many other gifts with which he has been blessed.

I did not forget patient number two. We found that it was not a stomach virus that was causing Aubrey to lose strength BUT blockages (four of them!!!). God blessed him, too, as he successfully had heart surgery, but that was not the last of his being kept. Later, a prostate cancer diagnosis and treatments were to follow, with which he is doing well. Thank You, FATHER, for keeping him/me/us!!! THANK YOU FOR THE YEARS THAT FOLLOWED AND THOSE STLL TO BE!!! God is pleased with us when we believe His Word and He will honor us with favor to be whom He created us to be, to do that which He created us to do. For this, I am sooo grateful!!!!!!!!!!!!!

Chapter 6

SOME *NOS* ARE A BLESSING IN DISGUISE

ALLOW ME TO ENCOURAGE YOU TO KNOW THAT ALL PLANS THAT DO NOT GO THE WAY WE'D HOPE ARE NOT NECESSARILY BAD PLANS/RESULTS. SOME OF THEM ARE GOD'S REDIRECTION SO THAT HE CAN BLESS US IN SOME AMAZING WAYS. I taught English briefly at S. H. Archer and George High Schools and for more than eighteen years at Harper High School, where I also coached forensics (especially debate) for ten years. When given this second assignment, I tried after a year or so to give it up, since I'd not heard of the program and what it entailed, but my principal, Mr. Irons, would not have it. And so, off I went to find out more about it (beyond treating it like "a club"), how to do it, and how to get others in neighboring high schools to join me in this quest. **I found another coach (Dr. Moss at Therrell HS) who**

was also seeking connectedness and another teacher (Miss Youngblood, Archer HS) willing to become a coach. Another teacher (Mrs. Geer, Washington HS) soon joined us. At that same time, Melissa Maxcy Wade, the Director of the Barkley Forum at Emory University, was beginning to develop an interest in assisting Atlanta Public Schools in developing a system-wide program. We sought her assistance and began to recruit students to participate on the city, state, and national levels, first through becoming a part of the establishment of the Atlanta Urban Debate League. We were soon allowed to seek scholarships for the ENDI, a summer debate program at Emory. Dr. Moss soon became Director of the Coaches Institute, and I became a dorm counselor. Very soon thereafter, we were competing at local, state, and national-level tournaments.

God began to BLESS US ALL, as students began to place in all level tournaments, and I was asked to become a Lab Leader at an institute in Miami, conferences in New York, and other cities where debate leagues were being formed using the Atlanta Urban Debate League model. What a blessing to have this opportunity to travel; to work, making a difference with students in other cities, too; to attend a coach's institute in Iowa with two of my debaters who, too, had received scholarships to attend the student division, further persuaded by them to drive us there. IMAGINE THAT!!! I had to call my principal and thank him for the opportunities that were afforded me by his decision not to allow me to bow out of sponsorship of our school's squad. I was so grateful for this opportunity to thank him before his later illness and resultant homegoing.

An added blessing for me was the opportunity to work with the students in Miami who were in a program designed for students one step away from incarceration. They were such a JOY to work with. My students in Atlanta and in Miami helped me to see that we have soooooo many students with such amazing potential who have lost sight of, or have never discovered, how amazingly talented they are. Through debate, I began to see grade- point averages and reading skills increase dramatically and confidence in oral presentation worthy of praise. At that point, I had begun to go to a couple of young men's homes, taking them out and taking them to school. Because of these types of concern, which increased my blood pressure, slowly but surely, I decided that I must do something else to make a difference.

Even though I felt that I was doing God's will there, too, confirmed by having been chosen Star Teacher four or more times—a student-driven award—and Teacher of the Year by my co-workers, I had to find a balanced way to do so. And God began to do a MIGHTY WORK on my behalf in that effort. And so, I moved forward in God's leading.

Betty Jessie Maddox

When I decided to leave teaching to find another way to make a difference, a fellow coach, Dr. Moss, suggested that I ask if I could coordinate the forensics program for the System since I knew the process and concern of the coaches. I did, they said "yes," and off I went! AMAZING!!! When my position coordinating forensics for our public-school system was unexpectedly phased out nine years later, after all associated with its success recovered from disappointment, we realized that God had another job (door) waiting for me a year away at Emory University. He provided work for me in the meantime as a tutor (helping a young lady to graduate on time) and as a forensics teacher to a private school's after-school program. Along the way, there were many opportunities to travel and teach forensics in many cities across the country. I taught in after-school forensics programs in APS middle schools, served as head dorm counselor at Towson University in Vermont, and worked with programs in Washington, New York, Marquette University, and other programs developed on the Atlanta Urban Debate League model. I was also BLESSED TO BE ABLE TO ASSIST MY BROTHER, Rev. Richard A. Jessie, in the development of a league in my hometown, Columbus, Georgia. I WAS ALLOWED TO MAKE A DIFFERENCE NOT ONLY AT HOME BUT IN MANY OTHER CITIES AS WELL. HOW AWESOME IS THAT?!!!!!!

Through my involvement in debate, I was able to visit the site of the Oklahoma City bombing, and New York after the 9/11 tragedy, places I might not have visited were it not for debate. God just keeps on pouring His GRACE INTO MY LIFE, ALLOWING ME BLESSINGS IN MY EFFORTS TO BRING HIM GLORY, HONOR, AND PRAISE THROUGH THESE OPPORTUNITIES TO HELP OTHERS ACCOMPLISH MANY SIGNIFICANT ACHIEVEMENTS. I was honored, too, receiving many awards, among them The Paul S. Slappy Award for Promoting Diversity in Debate, a Key Coach Honorary Membership in the Barkley Forum at Emory University, and membership in the Georgia High School Forensics Coaches Hall of Fame. I was also honored to receive a Humanitarian Award from Campus Life Division of Emory University, a Black History Month Award for Community Service at Ben Hill UMC, and many others. THAT HELPED ME TO CONTINUE TO ENCOURAGE OTHERS, MY CALLING, THROUGH PRAYER FOR THEM AND SERVICE TO THEM. AND FOR THIS, I AM SOOO GRATEFUL!!!!

Many of my debaters and others with whom I was able to work have now become lawyers, district attorneys, doctors, ministers, teachers, and so much more. There is one young man, Edward, whom I watched grow from a student in a communications class that I taught to joining the debate squad and becoming an award-winning debater. He had a partial scholarship to the University of Alabama, was a coordinator of a debate league in California, went back to Alabama upon request of the administration to coach debate, and then to Emory (where Melissa had already decided he belonged) as a coach, leading the squad to several historic national wins, and is now the Director of The Barkley Forum. TALKING ABOUT A HEART FILLED WITH GRATITUDE TO GOD, HERE'S ONE!!!!!!!!!!!!!! So many other debaters of my coaching years and other APS high schools are now being used to BLESS OTHERS: Kenya, Assistant DA in Washington and NY, and Nekia, Therrell, also Assistant DA; April, an administrator of DeKalb County Cancer Medical Center; Haneefah and Shawn, both lawyers (Shawn courted to become involved in politics in AZ); and others like Tann and Marcus, who are ministers; Chris, Mays HS and Ben Hill UMC, who also studied abroad and is now employed with the State Department; and Erik, a graduate of Georgia State University, who first joined my debate squad, as he admits, for social connectedness, BUT NOW, totally sold on its value, having served at many middle and high school tournaments and workshops, is an Ambassador with Emory's Outreach Program, the AUDL, working with students on all levels of forensic involvement. There are so many more lawyers, teachers, entrepreneurs, etc., many of whom I was blessed to mentor, like Robin, from middle school through application to the bar association last year. Others are, too, making their mark in many other fields, and **I'M SOOOO PROUD!!!**

Chapter 7

I/We Can Overcome, NO MATTER WHAT!

While I had those AMAZING EXPERIENCES, there are some experiences I'd choose not to have; however, God promises that, NO MATTER WHAT MAY COME MY WAY, I CAN OVERCOME, THROUGH CHRIST JESUS, NO MATTER WHAT!!! My first career choice was to become a nurse, but upon having a serious conversation with myself, I realized that if I had become a nurse with an emergency room assignment and someone was brought in in terrible shape, the staff would have to pick me up from the floor and treat me. And so, on to career choice number two, teaching.

Now, having said that, after sharing the challenges in the lives of my family members (giving Tee IV procedures, helping Aubrey with several procedures he had to continue once dismissed from the hospital, keeping tabs on Eric, and later, as I will recall, having to do IV procedures with Kirk), I had to have an inquiring conversation with God relevant to His equipping me for nurse-like duties anyway. I'm so glad that God has a sense of humor when we inquire. As I have been "Nurse Maddox" to Tee, then Kirk, Aubrey, and Eric, God was still in the business of continuing this assignment.

And so, on to nursing duty opportunity number four. Aubrey and I went on a short trip and left Kirk in charge of the home front. When we returned, Kirk was not in, but we did not consider his not being home to be cause for concern until we checked our messages and realized that one was from him and that he was in the hospital. He said not to worry, but that is difficult for a parent to do. We called and, given as much as he knew, gained his assurance that he was fine. Since it was late, we decided to go down the next day.

This was Kirk's fourth hospital stay, the second being a partial amputation of a finger as a result of an infection, further aggravated by his recent diabetic diagnosis. That went well but later he experienced a basketball injury, and they were concerned that he could have a limp because he was such a big man. But God was in the healing. He did not have any limp at all, and the anxiety attacks he experienced while recuperating soon disappeared. Though we had hopes that trip four would soon be behind him, it was not to be.

The concerns for diabetes and the heart issue were uppermost during this last hospital stay, some sixteen years later, when he was diagnosed to have evidence of an infection. A week or so after he was dismissed from the hospital, a day before we were to take him to the doctor for a follow-up check-up, Kirk went home to join his sister, whose homegoing we thought still caused him some sadness, as he'd hoped his marrow would have saved her from early death.

But, before Kirk's homegoing, God would make his last day with us such a "Kept Moment" for his father and me. I was participating in our Sanctuary Choir Messiah Concert when it began. As president of the choir, I was savoring the success of the concert as I arrived home only to have Aubrey come to the door and say, "Hurry, Lilbits, we've got to go to the hospital. They've already taken Kirk." Confused and afraid, we rushed to the hospital. As we waited, Aubrey reviewed the events of the past few hours. He showed me how God had been with them/him, and I'd come to realize that my desire that he not be alone for any long periods was a precursor, too, although he'd not really complained of anything except feeling a little tired. But back to God's assurances to Aubrey. He'd earlier helped Kirk to freshen up and while they were doing so, Kirk said, "You and Mama have been some great parents." Aubrey reminded him that I'd cooked what he wanted for dinner, and he'd had his usual great helping. He went to his room to watch the football game while Aubrey watched from our room, and they carried on a conversation about the plays that had been called. After the game, Aubrey surfed the channels for something else to watch, and that's when it happened. Aubrey stopped to listen to "The Ole Ship of Zion" as he watched Rev. Jasper Williams' service. He then heard Kirk fall out of his bed and ran in to see what was happening. When he called 911, he was told that there was an ambulance near them, on its way. He heard it even as they said so. How AWESOME was it that God would have him hear that song, at that time? Praise God!!!

While we waited at Grady, we prayed and prayed. The doctor came in to say that they were still working on Kirk, but there was only a faint beat. With the passing of hours, they'd be concerned about brain function, even if they could revive him. With that in mind, they wanted to know our wishes. I wanted to see Kirk, but I thought that I knew what he'd want. Given the previous anxiety issues and knowing that he would not want to be only alive in part, and what he'd think to be a burden to others, I knew what Kirk would want. So, we gave them permission to let him go. We later thought of the smile that his "partner in goodness" and he would have on their faces as they were reunited.

On the day of his homegoing celebration, though it rained cats and dogs, his friends were right there, serving as pallbearers, saying by their actions, "He ain't heavy, he's my brother." As Aubrey said, "Kirk was a good man, and his steps were indeed ordered by the Lord." I smiled as I thought of them and him. A few years earlier, when Kirk received a check for his injury, out of the pure goodness of his heart, he sent Mom more than a thousand dollars!! HOW AWESOME IS THAT FOR A YOUNG MAN TO DO?!!! God further ordered that his eyes be a blessing to someone in need. Kirk's first cousin, Shonda, shared on Facebook how she felt when she heard of his homegoing. Kam, too, felt led to write in tribute to him and their relationship during her early visits to our home and the encouragement that he had lovingly put in her heart. ALL OF THESE ARE WAYS THAT GOD KEPT ME/US THROUGH A DIFFICULT TIME. WAYS FOR WHICH WE WERE, AND CONTINUE TO BE, GRATEFUL!!! For about a week or two after Kirk's homegoing, each day our doorbell would ring, but when we'd go to the door, there'd be no one there. I soon realized what time of day it was each day. Then I just began to praise God for the "playful" Kirk. We just began to say, "Come on in, Kirk, you know you're here already, anyway." We'd then laugh, as we realized that it rang each day at the time that he would have been coming home from school. That was Kirk! I'm sure he and Tee laughed about that for a while.

Kirk—Anointed Teacher, Nurturer of the Young, reader, singer

Chapter 8

LED BY HIS SPIRIT

MY STORY AGAIN GAINS CENTER focus as I, one who took doctor visits seriously, decided to go to my primary to ask that she schedule me for an overdue colonoscopy. I'd begun to feel some level of concern for abdominal discomfort I was beginning to feel. The results were of no major concern, but the discomfort continued, and so I requested a CAT scan be done. However, what they suggested might be the cause and what was treated still did not completely relieve my concerns. With this, I requested a CAT scan again, and this time they listened and found that there was a sizable growth in my right kidney, for which the decision was made to remove the kidney as best practice, in case it was malignant. And so off to the hospital I went. After surgery, I was told that it was wedged between/against my ribs, but the surgeon was one who did not believe in removing ribs unless absolutely necessary. So he worked diligently to remove the kidney with growth intact without removing any ribs, and this is what I'd have wanted. THANK YOU, FATHER GOD, FOR KEEPING ME!!! EVEN WHEN I'M ANESTHETIZED, YOU KNOW MY HEART'S DESIRES. Even when You know what is needed before the doctors and move me in my spirit to continue to press for a CAT scan.

Later at church, someone asked if I'd completed my dialysis, to which I answered that I'd not had to take dialysis. THAT I'D NEED TO DO SO NEVER WAS EVEN A THOUGHT TO ME, UNTIL ASKED THAT QUESTION. AND NEVER AFTER. Later, someone else asked if I'd completed my chemotherapy, to which I answered that I'd not had chemo. AGAIN, THAT I'D NEED TO, NEVER WAS A THOUGHT TO ME, UNTIL ASKED THAT QUESTION, AND NEVER AFTER. I WANTED TO JUST SHOUT TO THE RAFTERS ON BOTH OCCASIONS. As I write this testimony, I am seven years removed from the surgery and have not experienced any problems relevant to the kidney that was cancerous. TO GOD BE ALL GLORY!!!!!!!!!!!!!!!!! Now to be disciplined in drinking more water and avoiding or limiting some of my most favorite foods, for which I'll need your prayers. But our daughter believed that "I can do all things through

Christ, who strengthens me" (Phil. 4:13). AND SO DO I!!!

God has not promised us that our lives would be free of challenges but that we would be able to overcome them through faith in Him, through Christ Jesus. And so, as you can see, challenges come and come and come, BUT hold on to FAITH IN GOD, THROUGH CHRIST JESUS!!!

My most recent challenge was the health and well-being of my mom, who was ninety-five years old in March of last year. She was BLESSED AND BLESSED in so many ways before her homegoing last June. First with long life, which had been free of any major medical concerns until the last two to three years. Even when she, my sister Aileen, and Aileen's daughter, Loretta, were involved in a VERY SERIOUS ACCIDENT, God protected them all in a mighty way. The major concern recently was loss of some memory. As she was one who loved her home, she had not wanted to entertain the idea that she could no longer live alone. But God moved my thinking and acted upon the heart of our younger brother, Richard, who lived in the same city and was leasing with the possibility of purchasing a home, to move in with her. Her doctor said that it would not affect her in a negative way if she'd visit us for at least a week of each month so that he, too, could have a period of time to himself. And so we decided that as long as she could visit us and be given support by Richard while home, that was the plan we would follow, allowing her the peace and comfort of home. When we began to think that Mom was experiencing her last days on earth, I went home to be with her that week, putting things in place at home so that Aubrey and Eric would be well until the weekend.

While there, I saw Mom become more and more aggravated by simple things, like not being able to go to the restroom. I tried to assure her that it was okay and that we'd take care of her. Yet, she was still not comfortable. This fine lady with class and dignity did not like that at all. I talked with God about it, and He assured me that all would be well. Although she could not talk much, she did say something that I was pretty sure was what I heard. She said, "I'm changing." I asked her what she'd said, and she repeated it. I asked her if that was what she'd said, to which she shook her head. Because of this, I decided to return home a little earlier to take care of concerns for Aubrey and Eric in preparation for my return to Mom's by Saturday, but that Friday morning, Mom went on to Glory to see her Father, Jesus, Tee, Kirk, and many other family members and friends who'd gone on before. It further amazes me, too, that she and I seemed to be on the same mental wavelength: we cut our hair to very short styles; had concern for kidneys (hers more minor) at the same time; developed a chronic cough at similar times, probably sinus related; needed to overcome the challenge of increasing water intake; some other instances of thoughts along the same line at the same time. AMAZING!

Chapter 9

Empowered by God's PEACE, His GRACE, and His MERCY

As I indicated, the Holy Spirit directed me to do this journey/narrative in testimony of how God has kept me sane, joyful, comforted, grateful, loving, reverent, and sooo much more. Many people wonder how I can be at peace with two children who have gone home, and my mom as well, how I can deal with all of our health issues that are now raising their heads, the affairs of our nation, and sooo much more. One piece of advice I'd give to everyone is to FILL YOUR LIVES WITH MANY, MANY MOMENTS/MEMORIES OF TIMES WITH THEM, OF HILARIOUS MOMENTS THAT REVEAL SOMETHING ABOUT THEM OR YOU. When you're tempted to feel overwhelmingly saddened, draw from your treasure trove of BLESSED MOMENTS AND BE GRATEFUL. As for **our mom**, she lived to be more than ninety-five years of age, and that in itself is SUCH A BLESSING, especially when some people have been without their parents since childhood or young adulthood, some always without parents. We often find ourselves quoting some of her famous beliefs. For example, she'd say, "God is still in charge," or when someone had accomplished something praiseworthy, she'd say, "Well, you came from great stock." When her granddaughters exercise their culinary skills and are praised, we recall that she would have been proud.

As for **Kirk and Tee**, had the doctor not done the cesarean section, we might not have had **Kirk at all. For the thirty-seven years that we had him here, we are grateful** for the memories; his academic accomplishments, having just completed his master's degree a year before his homegoing; his educational contribution to the Bankhead area elementary school children; his contribution to Ben Hill's children's summer programs; and the C. L. Henderson Male Chorus, in which he sang with his father and brother. We often recall how much he was afraid of almost everything in his early years—he who shook in his boots when he saw the Disney characters after looking forward to seeing them for weeks. We'd remember his love for wrestling; his love for superheroes (a love shared with his cousin Al); his love of books, often having to be awakened at the close of the library; his Dave & Buster's trips when something would trigger the recall; and the JOY. We'd remember how our nieces, especially Kam, and nephews (like Kort) would flock to his room as quickly as possible once we'd open the door when they visited. Young children had a sense of the type of spirit he possessed. **I AM SOOOOO GRATEFUL!!!**

Had I decided to have the tubal ligation, we would not have had Tee AT ALL, AND SOOO, PRAISE GOD!!!! **PRAISE GOD FOR THE EIGHTEEN YEARS OF JOY, ACCOMPLISHMENT, FAITH, CHARACTER, AND PERSONALITY OF TAZANYA!!!!!** I encourage you to read her story in my book published late last year, *She Graduated Early: from Earth to Glory*, honoring God's FAITHFULNESS FOR HER FAITHFULNESS. Soooo MANY have shared with me how BLESSED they were through reading her story. Many remembered her ministry through song, with the C. L. Henderson Male Chorus on one occasion, and especially "Over My Head," which MANY remember from the recording of her ministering it at her homegoing. Her strange vocabulary (e.g., "rubber meat" for some boiled ham pieces or "cold covers" for the feel of sheets) and other behaviors made us smile. That really does mean much to me, as I was led to write her story to encourage anyone from ten years to one hundred ten years to believe in God's FAITHFULNESS TO THOSE WHO WOULD TRUST HIM and find JOY IN SPITE OF LIFE'S

CHALLENGES. For that reason, I chose to write it in a reasonably short narrative, as if just talking to them.

God has kept, and CONTINUES TO KEEP, our oldest, Eric, in service to His people, through SOOO MANY areas where his talents and gifts have been such a **BLESSING to his community and his church, especially as he has worked with young people since his youth,** from involvement with children's community football to Boys R.I.S.E. and the Youth. The United Methodist Men, the Vision (Arts) Ministry, and the C. L. Henderson Male Chorus are ways that he contributes to adult ministries in the church. His artwork is **God-inspired,** from portraits to banners to program covers, etc. Eric also drew **AMAZING portraits of his siblings, including the cover for Tee's story.** Other evidence of his God-given talent is represented in an episode of *America's Most Wanted*, *Unsolved Mysteries*, and *In the Heat of the Night*. He and his work made a cameo appearance in *Those Bedroom Eyes*, a made-for-television movie starring Mimi Rogers, now appearing on *Court TV,* and as an illustrator for books by me, a friend, Stephen Randall, and his aunt, Elizabeth M. Hunley. **I THANK GOD FOR HIS SERVANT SPIRIT!!!!**

Oh, to be Kept by Jesus

Eric—Anointed Artist, Youth Leader, Singer

Chapter 10

To Encourage You, Too

Jeremiah 29:11–14; Isaiah 26:3, 55:11

As I approach the completion of this book, I am so grateful for this opportunity to share with you my testimony of how God has kept me in His GRACE and His MERCY!!! Sometimes when I think of my responses or reactions to situations, I know that it is God who has kept me in His perfect PEACE. As I asked why I do not respond to some situations even as I did in days gone by, He reminded me of my daily prayer that He will keep me in His perfect peace if I keep my mind stayed on Him and trust in Him, and I so choose.

I was kept (used/honored) by God during an exercise at a United Methodist Women Conference promoting our connection to one another and to God. We were told to repeat words of encouragement given by the narrator as we held the hands of other women in the circle. Following the exercise, the young lady to whom I'd spoken those words came over to me with tears in her eyes and confessed that she'd just gone through a tough divorce, but as I spoke to her, she felt and saw the love of Jesus in my eyes and was SOO encouraged therefrom. HOW AWESOME AN EXPERIENCE IS THAT?!!! I PRAY that all I do honors HIM.

I was further kept at that same conference when I slept well while others had trouble sleeping the NIGHT BEFORE THE MORNING THAT I WOULD HEAR OF MY BROTHER BEING SHOT. I prayed that I'd get there before Bernard's death in support of him, his wife and children.

GOD KNEW THAT I'D NEED REST FOR THE AFFAIRS OF THAT NEXT DAY. HE KEPT ME IN HIS PEACE AND STRENGTH. THANK YOU, FATHER!!!

God again kept me in His purpose when, about three years before Aunt Flora's homegoing at one hundred and three years of age, He led me to personally have her poetry copyrighted and then published with the help of Office Depot. I did the typing, added graphics, and had them bind it. When I presented it to her, she cried and commented that although she did not go to college as did her sister, she too, was now a published author. I had not realized that it was that important to her. She began to tell everyone about her poetry book. Thank you, God. I'm so glad that I followed the leading of your Spirit.

I was kept when at a restaurant I passed out from having choked on food, only to be revived within a short period of time with no feeling of discomfort or fear, as if I'd just dozed off for a second. I was kept in His JOY by being allowed to dance before Him and in ministry to His people at least three times through Inspired by God's Grace, a seniors' dance group formed before my surgery, increased nighttime travel concerns, and other family health challenges that now affect my participation. This group was envisioned by some of us—more than twenty years earlier—who are now seniors. **THANK YOU, FATHER, FOR ALLOWING US/ME TO PRAISE YOU AS I DANCED BEFORE YOU!!! I imagine that the day I come before you will be a day that I'll dance even more IN GRATITUDE. HALLELUJAH!!!** I could go on and on and on in recognition of, and thanksgiving for, such special moments of blessings in the safety of His PEACE and JOY.

But these are some of my many moments of being kept safe, kept in peace, and kept in the assurance of His promises and love. I pray for ways that I may bring Him glory, honor, and praise so that I am encouraged to continue on and on and on. Now, I hope that you, too, will be encouraged, too, when (even before) times are challenging, to look back at the many times that

Jesus has kept you, too, and will continue to do so. IF YOU BELIEVE, **"I KNOW THE PLANS I HAVE FOR YOU, NOT TO HARM YOU, PLANS FOR GOOD, A FUTURE WITH HOPE" (JEREMIAH 29:11–14),** and you know/believe that **"HIS WORD WILL NOT GO OUT AND RETURN UNTO HIM VOID BUT ACCOMPLISH THAT FOR WHICH HE PURPOSED IT" (Isaiah 55:11),** NO MATTER WHAT, **THEN BE REMINDED/ENCOURAGED THAT HE "WILL KEEP YOU IN PERFECT PEACE WHOSE MINDS ARE STAYED ON HIM AND TRUST IN HIM" (Isaiah 26:3).** IF THIS IS YOUR RESOLVE, **LOOK FOR HIS PEACE IN EVERYTHING THAT COMES YOUR WAY!!! FIND IT THERE!!! BE FURTHER ENCOURAGED BY IT!! PRAISE HIM FOR IT!!!! NO MATTER WHAT!!! NO MATTER WHAT!!! AMEN! AMEN! AMEN!**

TO GOD BE ALL GLORY, HONOR, AND PRAISE, AND TO YOU, I PRAY HIS BLESSINGS BEYOND YOUR GREATEST EXPECTATIONS AS YOU READ THE FOLLOWING PAGES!!!!!!!!!!!!!!!!!!

Often, just hearing from someone when we are challenged by life's concerns, or even when all is going well, can encourage us in the **"now"** or for a **time yet to come.** From the excerpt taken from Tee's essays to the poetry written especially for our mother to other poems written by me to strengthen the persons to whom I send them, I pray that you will find something that encourages your soul and causes you to grow in faith and receive more of the PEACE of God, in Jesus' name I pray. The pages that follow are my prayer to God through Christ Jesus, on your behalf.

YOUR SPIRITUAL TRUTHS

The Questions Are

Some words/thoughts that we read or hear cause us to pause and examine the truths of our spirit. What spiritual truths do you discover about yourself as you meditate on the following: **THEN WHAT?**

What Do You Say?
Some say, "He's never failed me, yet."
While others say, "He NEVER fails!"
WHAT DO YOU SAY???

REAL LOVE
God asks in His Word: "If a man say, I love God, and hateth his brother, he is a liar: for he that loveth not his brother whom he hath seen, how can he love God whom he hath not seen?" (1 John 4:20, KJV) **FOOD for SERIOUS THOUGHT.**

Betty Jessie Maddox

The Question Is
One songwriter asks, "You don't love God??!!
What's wrong with you??!!!"
(Your answer is…)?

Give serious thought if there are those spiritual questions that cause you to pause and utter a "Hmm?" OR, if you feel that you are NOT where God would have you be, for He would say, 6. "Do not be anxious about anything, but in every situation, by prayer and petition, with thanksgiving, present your requests to God. 7. And the peace of God, which transcends all understanding, will guard your hearts and your minds in Christ Jesus." (Phil. 4:6–7)

Excerpts from Tazanya deAnn Maddox's Essays
An insert (in Her Honor/Memory) in the United Methodist Women's
Mother/Daughter/Friend Luncheon Program
September 18, 1993

EDUCATION:
Education in public school is free, and getting one is our job as students, for which we get paid on the night we receive our certification that will serve as credentials for employment. (To which I'd add, take advantage of it,

seek to know your calling, and then, as Tee would say, **"Go forward!"**)

HEROISM:

The ultimate advice I have to offer is to be your own hero or heroine. This means, do something great in life, that will affect others. I know that you are probably saying, "I can't," **but say, "I can."** It takes time, effort, and education.

WHO AM I? MY PURPOSE?

I AM A CHILD OF GOD!!! I have been taught and believe that everyone is placed on this earth for a reason—my reason being to encourage others through my experiences and through song. I enjoy performing in special programs and at church. The lyrics in many of the songs may uplift the listener in his emotional and sometimes physical pain. God has blessed me tremendously in my ability to sing.

I value every aspect of my life because if I did not, I would be alive, NOT living!!! "I can do ALL things through Christ who strengthens me" (Phil. 4:13).

PLEASE NOTE: I HOPE THAT I HAVE BEGUN TO BLESS YOU BY NOW WITH THE UNDERSTANDING THAT GOD "KEEPS" US IN MANY WAYS WHEN THINGS ARE GOING RIGHT, TOO, ENCOURAGING US TO CONTINUE TO TRUST HIM. Sometimes it's with the desires of our hearts or something else that encourages us to trust for our PEACE, JOY, AND COMFORT. Last Friday, May 11, 2018, I decided to FINISH GOING THROUGH THINGS/BOXES, INCLUDING MY "KEEPSAKES," OLD BILLS, AND THOSE DOCUMENTS I CATCH MYSELF HOLDING ON TO FOR A GIVEN PERIOD OF TIME. GOD SOMETIMES KEEPS US THROUGH THAT, TOO, AS WE READ CARDS, REMEMBER PEOPLE WE'VE NOT SEEN FOR A WHILE, ETC. Yesterday, as I pulled out some old albums (the children at their younger years, Ben Hill UMC memories, I saw persons who are now in heaven or at another church, messages and cards at different points in life's challenges in our lives, pictures, programs of special notes (including the Maddox Family Day at Ben Hill that I'D MENTIONED EARLIER IN THIS TESTIMONY).

As I showed them to Aubrey, he began reading and found something that I guess I typed once I received it, BUT **I DON'T REMEMBER IT AT ALL.** I MUST SHARE IT, **AS IT BLESSED ME SO TODAY. NOW, I wish to bless you with it.** There are sooo many examples of Tee's artwork and poetry to her brothers, grandmother, Aubrey, me and others, but for so many other reasons, among them her loveeee for *Boyz II Men,* I am led to share this one with you and return to complete my mission with even more of a song in my heart.

Betty Jessie Maddox

THE START OF A ROAD

(To the tune of "The End of the Road")
We belong together
And you know that I'm right
You always lifted my problems
And made them so light.
Will be forever,
Our love could never die
When you leave the hospital
You're missed once you say "Goodbye."
When I can't sleep at night,
You make sure I'm fine.
You talk when I'm scared
And I'm instantly fine.
When there's a pain in my head
You pat on my neck
To make sure I don't have a fever.

Oh, to be Kept by Jesus

We have come to the start of a road.
You help me hold on
You're a natural.
I know you (love) me.
I thank God for you!
By Tazanya (Tee)
Written for my birthday, February 4, 1993
Typed by me (I guess), but I don't remember doing it.
BUT GOD!!!

Betty Jessie Maddox

Kept by Encouragement to One Another

FOR FURTHER SPIRITUAL ENCOURAGEMENT!!!

OUR PASTOR REMINDED US OF God's evaluation of His creation, as upon completion of each, God said, "That's good." Rev. Dr. Byron E. Thomas spoke of the relationship of one with the other, as He created all of creation to be intimately involved with each other. As our worship focus for that Sunday, he spoke of the intimate relationship between husband and wife. He suggested that **beyond the physical intimacy,** there is a deeper level of intimacy that God would have us develop, one that strengthens relationships in more sustaining ways.

As I revisited this to encourage us to look forward to that period in time when that intimacy will be evidenced across species of God's creation, it led me to these thoughts:

Sit quietly in a meditative posture. Allow the imagery that I paint to visit all of your senses, your spirit.

You are on a beach and you hear the rhythm, the music of the waves as they dance first, before your eyes. Allow it now to penetrate your ears, soothing your inner spirit and relaxing every part of your being.

You leave the beach and travel to another scene, an AMAZING snowy mountaintop, created by God. Listen to the sound of the birds as they communicate with one another and somehow communicate with you. Visit a valley low, a rainbow of flowers, a paintbrush of beautiful strokes, and listen to the breeze in the trees, the bees that buzz about with more musical messages to your spirit, much in the same fashion as did the waves of the water. Relax in their presence. **JUST REMEMBER THAT,** under certain circumstances, the relationship between oceans and man, birds, bees, and other living creatures, the mountain and a valley full of God's AWESOMELY BEAUTIFUL NATURE MEANT TO BE IN HARMONY, could represent much peril**, BUT WITH GOD…!!!**

NOW JUST IMAGINE: God's foreshadowing that the day will come when… "The wolf and the lamb will live together; the leopard will lie down with the baby goat. The calf and the yearling will be safe with the lion, and a little child will lead them all" (Isaiah 11:6). What an intimate relationship that describes when ALL will be in HARMONY/AT PEACE!!! **HOW AWESOME IS THAT!!! A PERIOD OF TOTAL PEACE TO WHICH GOD WOULD SAY, "THAT'S GOOD!!!"**

Betty Jessie Maddox

OUR MOTHER, A WOMAN OF VIRTUE

God made YOU and He said, "That's GOOD!!!"
He knew He could count on you to be all that you could.
A mother of four, so well-kept near His Word,
Knowing the good that He wanted you to impart to us,
You knew that which for our lives was a must.
He made you as strong as the oak tree,
For He knew there'd be trials that you could not foresee,
Yet He made you fragile to some degree
So that you would remember to look to Him
For those days and hours
When trials would come and threaten to devour.
What an awesome trust He gave to you,
And we are so thankful that you were fit for that test,
For God really did give us His BEST.
AND SO, we say, in affirmation to His creation of YOU,
"That's GOOD!!!"
My prayer for you this day
Is that there is NOTHING THAT WILL YOU DISMAY,

Oh, to be Kept by Jesus

That you will find JOY IN ALL TIMES,
That you will be more PEACEFUL with each passing day
And that He will protect you from all harm
AND REST WITH YOU, IN YOU, AND ALL AROUND YOU
FOREVERMORE.
I LOVE YOU MUCH, MOST, AND ALWAYS!!!

Betty Jean
To Mrs. Susie H. Jessie

Betty Jessie Maddox

TO OUR MOTHER: BLESSED AND A BLESSING!!!

(Mrs. Susie H. Jessie)

How can we begin to say what you mean to us all?
When we need you, all we have to do is call.
You always take our needs to heart,
Always there with wisdom to impart.
We are so BLESSED that God blessed you to be
Our Grandmother's Daughter, Our Mother, Mother-in-
Love, and Grandmother for all the world to see,

Oh, to be Kept by Jesus

For ALL the world to be BLESSED BY YOU as are we. We pray that our lives will mirror your love, integrity, strength of faith, and compassion so that others will be likewise blessed by us.
May this SPECIAL DAY bring you much JOY, PEACE, WHOLENESS, AND BLESSINGS BEYOND ANYTHING YOU COULD EVER IMAGINE!!!!!!!!!!
A VERY, VERY HAPPY MOTHER'S DAY, MOM!!!!!!!
MUCH, MUCH, MUCH LOVE AND GRATITUDE!!!!!!!!!!!

Aubrey, Betty Jean, Richard, Eric (Kirk and Tee)

A One Hundred and One Year Old BLESSING

Mrs. Flora Maddox Reid, affectionately called **Nan Nan** by her nieces and nephews, was born November 11, 1905. She comes from a musical family—founding the St. Cecilia Children's Choir for the St. Mark AME Church—and when she felt that her singing voice was beginning to fail as she turned seventy years of age, she taught herself to play the harmonica. What a magnificent choice of instruments. She also began to transfer the rhythm and rhyme of music to the writing of poetry and began to nurture that gift as well.

Nan Nan writes her autobiographical sketch in several of the poems submitted to this collection. The author of this "tribute" to her furthers her biography in several poems submitted and dedicated to **Nan Nan**, who has dedicated so many poems herein to persons and places she desires to honor or praise.

Nan Nan's FAITH in and **LOVE** of **God** are very obvious when you read her poems **PRAISING** Him, Jesus, and His Holy Spirit, who often prompts her to give spiritual advice or words of wisdom to those of us who must "walk where she's walked" many years ahead of us.

Because **Nan Nan** has been preceded in her heavenly homegoing by her husband, Henry, her daughter, Thelma, her granddaughter, Curlye, her six siblings, and many other younger relatives and friends, she often wonders why God has blessed her with such longevity and an active life (still driving until she was ninety-five years old). To you, **Nan Nan,** I'd say, God honors your faithfulness to Him, Jesus, and His Holy Spirit, and He honors your self-sacrificing nature as you have served and continue to serve Him by serving others—family, friends, and so many others—bringing Him honor in all that you do. The visits and calls to the sick and shut-in members of your church and family were true BLESSINGS!!!

This is your season to enjoy, Nan Nan!!! There are many more poems for you to write. **WRITE ON!!!** He will give you strength to continue to play your harmonica when someone needs to be encouraged therefrom. **PLAY ON!!!**

I pray that God will bless you with many more years of LIFE, JOY, STRENGTH, LOVE, PEACE, FAITH, and PRAISES to Him, who has kept and will continue to keep you.

This collection of your poems is my gift of LOVE to you, Nan Nan—a name I'm SO HONORED to call you!!!!

Betty (your niece-in-LOVE)

Betty Jessie Maddox

PLEASE ENJOY, BE ENCOURAGED BY NAN NAN'S POEM
(One of her shortest BUT SO FULL OF ADVICE)

ONE ROSE

When I've crossed the swelling tide
With Heaven in my view,
Don't purchase a rose garden
Just one rose will do.
I've tried to grow my flowers
While living here with you.
I've tried to help you understand

Oh, to be Kept by Jesus

Why just one rose will do.
While traveling life's highway,
Slow down and think things through.
Do less talking and listen
And just one rose will do.
Just show your love for others;
Always be kind and true.
Be swift to lend a helping hand
And just one rose will do.
Flora Maddox Reid

NOTE: Aunt Flora passed two years later at the age of one hundred and three. WE HONORED HER DESIRE FOR JUST ONE ROSE.

THE BLESSING THAT BLESSES

A STRONG WOMAN OF GOD-
Full of grace, wisdom, and mirth;
To others she always gives a nod.
That's why one hundred plus years on earth
Are a part of her God's reward.
God needs someone who will affirm
Those who are struggling with daily fare
To say to them that God and she both care,
To keep the faith and run their race

Oh, to be Kept by Jesus

For He will not allow more than they could face.
But they must trust Him and never doubt,
Seeking His will each and every day,
For therein is the BEST way out.
She has already traveled many of the roads that we now tread.
She has climbed many mountains of seemingly
unreachable heights.
Her valleys have been full of tall grass and sod
But she made it through each looking to God for His light.
So to whom else could He best entrust His Sacred Word
But one whose testimony is true,
That God will always see you through?
So this is why she loves him so
And we love her more than she'll ever know.
So this is why she plays for Him,
And gives a nod to those who need to know
That she, with Him, love them so.
Keep on praising Him with your harmonica, Aunt Flora,
That second instrument of praise He blessed your
prayer to give,
Has many more years, we pray, with you to live.
He is pleased with all that you have allowed Him to
bless through you
And He will, without a doubt, continue to bless you, too.
Still We 5: Aubrey, Betty, Eric, Kirk (and Tazanya, too)
(Included in the dedication of her poetry book, *Blessed to Be a Blessing*)

Betty Jessie Maddox

Monday, December 14, 2009
Kirk,

I read you died today on Facebook.
I'm driving down the road
Thinking of the past.
Heavy now is my load;
Your life went by so fast.
Such a simple man
Who always did things his way.
Just when your life began
You left, though we wanted you to stay.
You were such a brilliant light
Extinguished far too soon.
Your calling—molding young minds so bright—
Taught to shoot for the moon.
I know that you can't come back,
Regardless of how hard I wish or try.
For now you are in Heaven,
As an angel standing by.

Love,
Shonda

December 14, 2009
My Dear Cousin,
It feels like yesterday when your mom would come and pick me, Kortland, and Sef up from school. As soon as I got to the house, I would race upstairs to your room and find you lying on the bed watching *106 & Park* or *Sanford and Son*, and as soon as I'd walk through your door, you would say, "There goes my buddy." I would just smile and join you while you watched TV. I could always count on you to get a genuine smile out of me no matter how I was feeling or how my day had gone. I remember you telling me about the children in your class and about how you constantly had to confiscate things from them because they were always playing with toys, CDs, crayons, and everything in between. You would always tell me that you wanted me to come to clean and decorate your classroom, and I would tell you that one day I would come and do it.

It just seems unfair; you left before I got to tell you how much I love and care for you and how much you mean to me. I remember when I would ask you a million and one questions, and you would answer them all with a smile. You would always tell me facts about different

TV shows, and I still remember them. I will never forget the day you asked me what Fred Sanford's real name was and when I yelled out, "Redd Foxx!" you were shocked and said, "I knew you were smart, Little Cousin." You watched me transition from elementary school to middle school and from middle school to high school. It's so hard for me to believe that you are really gone. My mind and heart won't let me digest that thought yet. Remember when you took Kortland to the prom and I wanted to go but he was mad and didn't want me to go? But you stepped in and said, "Come on, Kort, let your little sister go. It's not going to hurt." I will never ever forget you, and you will always have a place in my heart.   Kam I Am

Love,
your Little Cousin,
(Kam-I-am)

THE GIFT OF THE ROSE OF SHARON

We have been mandated to pray for one another;
That's what **God** would have us do
For those **He** has given us, each sister and brother.
And that we've done from day to day
Even when we have failed to write or call to say
That we care about you
And all of life's challenges that have visited you, too.
And by **His Spirit, God** prompted me this day
Just to write this note to say
A word of encouragement to you as you go along your way.
May you be reminded with each breath
That you take that the **ROSE of SHARON, Christ Jesus**, our **Lord**
Would have you remember the purpose of His death.
So shout, **"HALLELUJAH, the VICTORY IS ALREADY MINE!!!"**

Betty Jessie Maddox

NOW, **walk in the newness that is ALREADY thine,**
For the period of suffering, <u>if not yet</u>, WILL SOON BE LEFT BEHIND!!!
We further pray that **God,** our **Father; Jesus Christ**, our **Lord** and **Savior;**
and the **Holy Spirit, our Comforter** and **Counselor**
will dwell in you
RICHLY, BLESSING YOU, AND KEEPING YOU IN PEACE,
LOVE, AND JOY!!!

In the Flawless Love and Beauty of the Rose of Sharon,
We Pray, Aubrey, Betty, Eric (Kirk and Tazanya "Tee")

Oh, to be Kept by Jesus

BECAUSE WE DO CARE ENOUGH!!!

Just to let you know that you and your family
Are still thought of in prayer this day.
We pray that your connection to The Vine
Will allow His PEACE and LOVE
To surround you and comfort you in this time of
sorrow.
Know that we stand ready to assist you in any
way possible, and we pray that
Just as we share your sorrow,
We will share your Joy <u>that will come in the
morning.</u>

Lovingly connected to you and Him,
Aubrey, Betty, Eric (Kirk and Tee)Maddox

Betty Jessie Maddox

Just wanted to let you know that we are here,
ready to love on you and listen whenever you need it.

BECAUSE WE DO CARE ENOUGH...

We pray that the *POWER* of the *ROSE OF SHARON* will manifest healing in EVERY aspect of your being that is bruised or infirmed. IT IS YOURS ALREADY!!! BELIEVE IT!!! RECEIVE IT!!!.... JUST WAITING TO BE MANIFESTED IN THE EARTH...

The beauty of these roses does not compare to the beauty and power that Christ Jesus (the ROSE of SHARON) embodies.

Betty Jessie Maddox

May the warmth of His beauty, love, and power bring you strength of FAITH for this day's BREAD, for this day's journey. LOVE, PEACE, AND JOY ALWAYS,

We 5 Maddoxes

Oh, to be Kept by Jesus

HE IS RISEN AND SO ARE YOU!!!

From the point of mankind's sin,
God activated His plan for our redemption.
He told of the coming of Jesus, His only Son,
Who experienced our earthly conditions—for our eyes,
To show us that from which we, too, could rise.
Born in such a lowly state,
Respected not by those in His own land,
Tempted by Satan and other foes,
Felt betrayed by His Father
BUT empowered by the Holy Spirit

Betty Jessie Maddox

To overcome even in such times as those.
Because He overcame, so can we.
Believe what He has promised in His Word,
Recorded to encourage us along this path
That leads to Home.
"It (the Word) shall not go out and return unto me void
BUT accomplish that for which it was intended."
What an awesome promise to us!!!
Believe it!!! Walk in it this and every day!!! NO MATTER
WHAT!!! Rebuke the devourer with it!!!
HE IS RISEN AND SO MAY YOU
Rise above whatever circumstances have challenged your way.
NO MATTER WHAT!!! NO MATTER WHAT!!!
BE ESPECIALLY BLESSED WITH HEALING,
PEACE, AND JOY THROUGH YOUR
CONNECTION TO THE VINE ON THIS
SPECIAL DAY THAT HE HAS MADE FOR YOU
TO REJOICE AND BE GLAD!!!

Lovingly connected to You and Him,
The Maddoxes

www.ingramcontent.com/pod-product-compliance
Lightning Source LLC
Chambersburg PA
CBHW061803070526
44586CB00023B/2697